Ubiquitous Poetry
and
Motivational Quotes
by
Jawusky

Peace Love and Prosperity
Copyright © 2017 Jawusky Mayfield
All rights reserved
ISBN: 978-0-692-93885-0

DEDICATION
To All the Poets Readers
Artists and Everyone
Around the World

Table of Contents

Introduction 5

Peace Love and Prosperity 6

Peace 7

Believe 15

Dream 21

Love 31

Inspire 43

Beauty 57

Change 71

Power 75

Perception 79

Life 85

To Be 93

Bonus Poems 105

About Me 111

Introduction

Hi. I'm Jawusky Mayfield. I am an artist. I create music, art and poetry. But most importantly, one thing I have learned within my lifetime is you can do anything you put your mind to, and staying positive is also a big factor in being successful.

Yes. I am an Average Joe, nothing greater and nothing less. But what I do know is this…Everyone has the potential to be great and achieve beyond one's wildest dreams.

One of the tools I use for expressing this message is my poetry. Poetry is a wonderful outlet for feelings and emotions. It can also show people that are going through some sort of obstacle that they are not alone. So I created this book to remind you that you are not alone, and everyone struggles through something. But staying focused, believing and not giving up will determine if you are successful or not.

Motivational Quotes

Peace Love and Prosperity

    This book has something for everyone from all walks of life to relate to. My goal is to show empathy and to motivate you to be your greatest self, and to remind you, even in your lowest times; you are greatness.

    So with that being said, enjoy the quotes and poetry I have put together and always remember:

You are amazing,
you are greatness,
and most importantly,
You are worthy.
Peace Love & Prosperity!

--Jawusky

PEACE

Identify your emotions.

Monitor your thoughts.

Analyze your words

before you speak them.

-- Jawusky

On My Search for Peace

As I travel through my mind
On a quest for this state
Hills and mountains I climb
But never shall I lose faith

I see it from a distance
As it fades farther and farther away
And the riot begins
But I still continue to pray

As I travel the world
From state to state
Sounds of existence follow me
From place to place

From the depths of my mind
These noises orchestrate
And the riot goes on
As it grows day by day

Ubiquitous Poetry

***

*The more experiences I go through,
the slower I am to judge
the next person because I never know
what that person has been through
to lead them to that conclusion.*

--Jawusky

***

The Garden of Souls

I've never witnessed the comfort
Of a warmth so behold
Soft whispers of eternity
So familiar to my soul

Held by the hands of mystery beyond time
With a consciousness swayed by the winds of love in euphoria
Like a baby in the arms of his mother
Getting sleepier
And sleepier
Only to dose deeper
And deeper
Into the garden of souls

Ubiquitous Poetry

***

Man, like the moon, has many faces.

--Jawusky

***

Mother Nature

In love with travel
Exploring the sacred body of Mother Nature
She is food and candy to the eyes
Of my soul
I often find myself
At a lust for her beauty
Into the way she makes me feel
I feel as if I've died amidst every eyegasm
And resuscitated to life
All in one moment
At the sight of you
You are so beautiful

I Will Not Forsake

I will not forsake my brother
No matter his race
Creed
Or color
I will do my best to help
Though I must protect myself
I will not forsake my brother
All we have is each other

I will not forsake my sister
And leave her behind
I must offer my best guidance
When her sense may seem blind
I will remind her
Of her inner beauty and design
And where the energy flows
If she seeks
She will find
I will not forsake

Motivational Quotes

***

*Worry not.
The more you worry about it,
the more it's going to worry
You.*

--Jawusky

***

BELIEVE

If you fail today, try again tomorrow.

And if you fail again tomorrow,

don't be sad because you tried your best.

And trying your best is winning.

You are a success. You can do it.

Believe.

--Jawusky

A Man without Faith

A man without faith
Is like a key without a safe
Burdened by the stress of feeling worthless in the face of fear
Praying and hoping for his vision to become clear

With a clarity unrevealed
Let alone come near
It drifts farther and farther away into a vortex of disbelief
Subsequently comes the anguish
The pain
The grief

Feeling trapped and held captive behind walls of concrete
That can be waved in illusion
If you set your mind free

Keep Writing

3:22 am
And I'm counting sheep
My conscious fails to frizzle
As I toss and turn in my sheets
The light remains dim
But my thoughts remain brightened
So in my attempt to sleep
I began writing

As I continue on
My abyss goes deep
And my mind comes to float
Grasping the first thought I see
My pen begins to travel
Like a ship in the open sea
Without fear of losing grip
And holding on to a part of me
I'll keep writing

Protected

Worry not of hands
Or looks that fade away
Or weariness of fear
At the illusion of one's weapons

This intangible method
Is an everlasting connection
To a matter that is untouched
Un tampered ripple of progression

Stress not upon worries
Life's unanswered questions
All seeming to lack relevance
By god as my protection

***

*If you can believe, you'll be showered
with blessings that you can't believe.*

--Jawusky

***

Push Forward

Push forward
When times get tough and you feel like you can't make it
When it hurts inside and you just want to give up
You must push forward

When everyone around you is depending on you
But your mood is gloomy and your feeling is sad and blue
When you feel as if you failed to tap in to the light in you
There is nothing else to do
But push forward

You are the greatest
I know you will make it
Small thing to a giant
I know you can take it

This energy within you is something sacred
You have everything you need
To push forward

Motivational Quotes

***

If it happens in your mind,
it's already a reality.
But if you believe in it and work towards it,
it will manifest in front of your eyes.

***

Be careful of the words you speak.
They can bring success or failure.
Be positive.

***

Never disbelieve.
You are worthy.
If you weren't, you wouldn't BE.
You are worthy.

--Jawusky

***

DREAM

Believe and act upon your dreams.

And watch them come into fruition.

Let your dream be that of a brighter future

amongst the blessings of all in creation.

Dream.

--Jawusky

Often I Dream

Often I dream
In the realm of the unseen
Through the light of insight
My soul has given me

Often I dream
Of what it means to be free
When I close my eyes
And let my inner thoughts be
To another reality
With a visualization
Painted so vividly

Ooh how I began to see
This portrait of eternity
How could one explain
How it feels to be free

Picking up the Pieces

As I take a moment of silence
For those who passed way
For the endearment of our people
Moving forth to a brighter day
I find myself selecting pieces to pick up
And ones to put down
That will help us lift up
In the direction of progression
With the attitude of gratitude
Never forget about those that carved a path for you

I pay homage to the ones who put their lives on the line for me to see a better life

Through this liberating change
You are not forgotten
Your actions were not in vain
In a society gone rotten
Some may say it's the articulation of a genius
But along with being me
I call it picking up the pieces

Motivational Quotes

***

And poof
I am
As you are
And together
We are imagination

--Jawusky

***

It's More Than a Dream

It's more than a dream
The dream is real
As the ocean waves at night
And the lighthouse upon the hill

Sparks of light
And the most beautiful fright
To cause a twinkle in one's eyes
In the blink of oblivion

It's more than just a dream
As odd as it may seem
It's shivering delivery
May give your bones chills
Beyond what you see smell and hear is what you feel
And it's so close I can taste it
This dream is so real

Motivational Quotes

***

Be greatness.
You have the power within yourself
to attain beyond your wildest dreams.

***

Close your eyes,
Jump in your imagination,
See new places,
Take road trips.

***

Who needs movies
when you can edit the scenes
of your imagination?

***

Make your life a beautiful mandala.
Let your spirit guide you
upon the canvas of existence.

--Jawusky

***

I Write to Express

I write to express
I write to release
The path to create
The bridge for peace
Grab the pen and write the scrolls of your life
For your surroundings and those after you to see
What's new under the moon to see
As the sun shines
The pain from deep beneath
Forms into an upward seep
Spiraling down from my mind to the blank sheet of triple darkness

To bring movement upon life
May these writings shed light
Behind closed eyes lies everything in sight

Motivational Quotes

***

Dreams are like clairvoyant insights and answers to questions you ask yourself. The answer is already inside of you.

***

*Trace your dreams with feeling through your imagination
and paint your reality with faith.
Persistence and action upon life's canvas can
create a beautiful picture.*

***

*Don't give up.
You are one decision away from the life of your dreams.
Take your time, relax, breath and move forward.
Everything will work out fine.
Be positive.*

--Jawusky

***

Universal Kite

I send a kite through the stars that shine bright
So you can see through the darkness
That expounds the night
For the tribe of the lost and abandoned
I am your connection
You are no longer stranded
With infinite potential
To tap into
And illuminate the planet with

I send a kite
For the souls
Of the gone and forgotten
That your names create change through these youthful fountains
It is because of you we're able to shape these mountains

I send a kite as a shooting star across the sky
When one fades away
Another spark's nearby
The fulfillment and astonishment of the electric eye
Let it navigate the winds
Keep your head held high

I send a kite to my brothers and sisters locked in jail
Creating freedom throughout thoughts
In the restriction of a cell
If you're down and lost
and you feel like nobody cares

I send a universal kite
When I light these flares

I send a universal kite

Motivational Quotes

***

Be at peace with your mistakes.
For they are only proof of your belief
that your dream will take proof into physical reality through persistence.

***

Shine through your haters!
So bright that your light cleanses their being
and illuminates their soul! Shine!

--Jawusky

***

LOVE

And after the worldly ways

began to fade amongst its pains,

Love was without a blemish

And forever it shall remain

--Jawusky

We Are One

We are one
From the light of which we have become
From the source of the sun
To our mother who gave birth

We are one
With empathy and understanding
Unconditional love and compassion
Your pain becomes mine
Through every sound from the drops of rain splashing

Vibes and interactions
When it's all said and done
And everything else collapses
This love is everlasting
We are one

Sweet Lady

So beautiful
You are
O so graceful
I fantasize of you
May I taste you

Will you
Let me
I wonder
How many licks will it take for you
To come to me
Sweet Lady

Motivational Quotes

Love Is

Love is
The connection
Between me and you
Love is the open sky
And the waters clear blue
The drive to strive
To stay alive and survive
The compassion of the living
And the poverty stricken mind

The hope of the strain child
Giving
Though he was deprived
Even when he has nothing
He will lay down his life
Through all the hurt
Through all the hate
Even when barred down by the world's heavy weight
He will forever be by your side

The sound of soothing melodies of blues and smooth jazz
Love is ever so patient
It never moves too fast
 It is healing
The timeless quality that gets you by
Love is everlasting
Love is you and I
Love is

Love's Soldier

He who loves hard without using his brain
Cries tears of injustice
Accompanied by his pain
Consumed by his misguidance
In a past life was slain
Fool him once shame on you
A soldier of love he became

He who loves hard
Without using his brain
Wears his heart upon his sleeve
In this song of sorrow he sings
On his knees in the rain
With his face to the ground
The beautiful monster he became
Love's Soldier

Colors of Love

Sweet colors of love
Brushed softly upon her canvas
In motions of acrylic lust
With each stroke
My heart dances
Every flower is a kiss
From the passion of my soul
As a two dimensional painting
Identified as a rose
As the sensuality grows
Each practice becomes tantric
Every move becomes sexy
Birthing irresistible antics
Light a flare to your portrait
May it forever shine bright
As the reflection of the sun
Into the tapestry of the skies at night
We make love

Irresistible

The sound of her heels
Gives my soul warm chills
Like dark matter
Wrapped around my heart
Squeezing my vulnerability with her dominance
And intense coils with a mind of their own
Poisoned by her perfection is my imagination
Hypnotized by her perfume to do as she may please
Pulling me close as the earths gravitation
Her love is inevitable
A slave to the very utterance of her voice
As if I haven't a choice

Tranquilized by her touch
She takes my breath away with a kiss
Of sensational bliss that leaves me at a loss for words
I am hers
And she is my universe
Without her
There would be no me
She is my everything
Irresistible

Motivational Quotes

Cosmic Love

Through the invisible strands
From the stars above
So close
But yet so distant
We make cosmic love

From every atom of you
To every molecule within me
We create a big bang
In between universal sheets

Through the sun and the moon
Which comes in rotation
Each star holds a mesmerizing melody and vibration
Of cosmic love

Oh Maharishi

Inhale deeply
Exhale wisely
As we dive deep
Into the waters of the infinite mind

Holding hands with forever young
Playfully in a field of flowers
The sun laughs and giggles
Glitter sprinkled by fluffy white clouds
And magical moisture trickles

Where the body remains balanced
The spirit lies untouched
And the fog unveils the mystery
As the mountains remain hush

Peace
I come in peace
In all naturality
Of a flower that blossoms with no desire to contend

Visualize a crystallized state
From a purified love
Shaping and designing the most beautiful
Rock and diamonds of eternity

Everlastingly bold for the infinite mold
In the cold and still extends nothing other than love
O Maharishi

Angel of Music

I saw an angel
Her wings were enormous
Her entry was like
The most beautiful performance
Landing elegantly as if she floated towards me
Gliding
Delicately
Seducing my soul
I was hooked
Immeasurably
Then I'd levitate heavenly
As many moments passed
I would began to see melodies differently

I welcome you to the world
Of this angelic symphony
And lovely vibration
Where every song is an epiphany

Universal Love (The Beach)

Not often do we come across a love of this nature
A feeling of such healing
To come across this flavor
So beautiful I can taste her
As a pomegranate so sweet
Her waters are of purity
Diving in an everlasting sea
I arise where the land meets
As she glistens upon me

Where the moon illuminates truth
I stand upon beach land
The abundant grains of sand slowly seep in between the fingers of my hand
I star gaze upon you
For you are beautiful
Yes
You are beautiful
And I reflect
As your man
My love

Motivational Quotes

***

*As long as the thought is impressed
upon your mind,
it will perpetuate an existence.
Now, whether you think it's real, fake, true or false,
it is up to you to decide the properties
of your belief in the idea
impressed upon you.*

--Jawusky

***

INSPIRE

Write like someone is looking

and that someone is depending

on you

to inspire him or her

to be great.

--Jawusky

Motivational Quotes

We Are the Ones

How dare you speak hatefully toward my kind
In the defense of the same knowledge
Which robs you blind

Shame on your thoughts of stopping our shine
In defense of the same knowledge
That robs you blind
We are the ones

***

In order to be your own doctor,
you have to have patience.

***

Outer space is my mind
Each planet is a thought
Every star is a bright idea
And I am ...the galaxy

--Jawusky

***

I AM...

I am love
I am understanding
I am eternal
I am unique
I am great
I am healthy
I am perfect
I am inspiration
I am energetic
I am wealthy
I am for you…

I am the miracle
I am music
I am poetry
I am compassion
I am positive
I am spiritual
I am aware
I am kind
I am awake
I am darkness
I am connected
I am protected

I AM YOU…

Motivational Quotes

**

As I walk the earth
With the world on my back
From the weight on my shoulders
With each step
The surface cracks

***

Be encouraged.
Have the courage
to live your dreams
and be the person
that you want to be.
Be encouraged.

--Jawusky

***

Keep Straight

Keep straight
Stand strong
Never give up
Hold on
Move forward
I am with you
For you are not alone

I am the voice that calls your name
That you seem to recognize
I am the spirit here to guide
Though sometimes you never mind
You are not alone

Fear not
For you are protected
When you feel down on luck
Take a look at the stars
Let my hand pull you up

Morning noon and night throughout your life
I am the friend by your side
Synchronistic by sight
I am the orb in thin air
Crystalized under Heaven's light
I AM WITH YOU

Motivational Quotes

***

Magnify and compliment

the strong points in others

while standing with.

Belittling can only expose your insecurities

of feeling below another.

***

Don't worry;

it's not worth it.

You are worthy,

not worthless.

--Jawusky

***

My Inspiration

Where the rain pours loudly
And the skies get cloudy
Your inner light still glows
Stick your chest out proudly
And move forward
When you're down and out
And surrounded by darkness
With one look up
Here is my hand
I will help you up
Walk with dignity
Learn from your mistakes
Expand your understanding
See your goals and keep straight
There is always a way
To alleviate the heavy weight
So believe
remain strong
Be godly and keep faith
Believe in yourself
There are endless possibilities to the things you can do
It's amazing how much you can accomplish being you
Together we must continue
Beside you I will stand
The power is within you
My inspiration

Motivational Quotes

***

*We are imagination,
as the Aurora Borealis is,
Amazing.*

***

*Another great morning
is another great opportunity
to dive into the ocean
of infinite possibilities.*

***

*Always remember
how amazing you are.
Not because I told you to.
But because you are to be,
Amazing*

--Jawusky

***

Genius

Thinking
In the mind of a genius
The foolishness
Taunts me as I see it
I scrutinize the situation
And the way I perceive it
Then grace the scene
With a stroke of pure genius

Thinking
In the mind of a genius
Deep in the abyss
Sparks of electricity exist

I close my eyes
As I begin to envision
Images too advanced for theatres
Take a seat in your mind
Watch your own motion picture
Watch the scenes
And improv with no scriptures
I am the melody
Letting off intriguing sound
Naturally
Through the vibrations
Of a profound galaxy
As I tap at each star
In the constellation of keys
I display music
Orchestrated from the Heavens

Motivational Quotes

That flow through me
I am genius

***

If you don't like your current state of mind,
don't focus on it. Go to another state.
You are not a mountain. You can go other places.

***

It's good to reflect
upon your past thinking.
Because you're past thinking
helps create your present.

***

If you can't do a lot,
at least do a little.
Because after while,
you will have a magnificent
painting for the world to see

--Jawusky

***

The Continuance

Keep going
Sort of like the ocean
And the tides against the walls
That splash to keep the flow in
The reward of consistence
Adequacy and persistence
Your whole life and reality
Can change
Within an instance
Courageous
Bold
Relentless and fearless
The train that won't stop
But undoubtful of its weariness
The motion
The rhythm
The inevitable sequence
From a frequency resonated
By a stroke of pure genius
The sound between matter
That makes the rock solid
The radiance of the rays
Presented in ultra violet
Compulsive silence
Surrounding the meant to be
As the pieces we pick up
To recreate history
Through the science of mystery
As we move forth continuously
The continuance

Motivational Quotes

***

Never give up!
You can do it!
You can turn the dry lands into the Botanical Gardens!

***

The way to the promise land,
Where all places are magical,
Can be as easy as self-observation and the way you direct your attitude.

***

Lead by the example of greatness
to make your world a better place.
And by that example
your vibration will cause a ripple effect
throughout the worlds of others.

Your presence is felt more than you know.

--Jawusky

***

Distant Lover

I never knew
From so far away
Your understanding becomes stronger
When you hear my art speak
Our tentacles become warm
When were in arms reach
When we touch
It's a combustion
Like a volcanic eruption at its peak
We preserve charms speech so when trials become bleak
Our memories bring warmth
And comfort in the form of a quilted sheet
As time seeps through our fingers
As the sands at the beach
There will never be another
You will forever be with me
Distant lover

Motivational Quotes

We Are One (part 2)

We are one
From the same connection
Of the same source
Releasing different expressions
Spiritual monuments
Rounded in the same collection
To the same
we belong
Though we are not our possessions
Linked into an invisible thread
Which keeps us together
Cut from the same cloth
Torn from the same texture
From no boundaries of love
With the smoothness of a dove
Together we make elegance
As a feather dropped from above
As a hand to a glove
We are the perfect fit
Together we create memories
Though some fade in the midst
And still linger through time
As the flashes of one mind
I give thanks to all
For we are all one of a kind
Orchestrated through divinity
With a touch of pure beauty
And universal wonder
We are one

Ubiquitous Poetry

BEAUTY

If you only had a clue

how beautiful you are

rarely would you gaze

at the comparison of a star

--Jawusky

Motivational Quotes

Beauty in Its Purest Form

Beauty in its purest form
Gentleness in its lightest feather
The blessing of love
To touch hearts with the slightest effort
The definition of positive
With the smile of a queen
The light that never flickers
With a presence felt and seen

The essence of my being
For nine month's she carried me
The vision when I couldn't see
I am but a reflection of thee

Overwhelming joy
She created me to be
A child held to the sun
Which forever shines on me

That is Beauty

Beautiful

Sometimes I wonder
Of the softness of your lips
As the world begins to change
Each second from every kiss

When I hold you in my arms
Your feelings become mine
And you clinch me even tighter
As my thoughts enter your mind

And our bodies reunite
As souls intertwined
We ascend to lighter beings
In an intimacy beyond time

Show me your nakedness
And I will show you my compassion
Together we'll be forever
With a love that's everlasting

Motivational Quotes

***

Relax and observe.
Only to burst into the open space,
leaving manifestations of cosmic beauty
for the world to see.

***

By watering seeds of thought
that have been planted,
you create the flowers
for your garden of life.
Make your garden
beautiful and inspiring.

--Jawusky

***

Untitled Beauty

Her eyes were heartbreak
With a presence called love
Nothing less of a reminder
There is a Heaven above
Her smile is like poetry
When she laughs
My eyes listen
When she speaks
My heart skips a beat
For my soul is at her attention

Motivational Quotes

Happy Mother's Day to All

As the blossoming of the trees
And the scent of fresh flowers fragrance the Earth

Is the likeness to the beauty
Of the mother that gives birth

Springtime is the miraculous
Expression of love and life
given by moms all over the world
For you are beautiful
I wish you
A Happy Mother's Day

The Hummingbirds Rock

For summer's delight
Beauties messenger swoops to astonish man
With universal artistry fluttering in place
As timeless candy for the eyes to taste

Flashing rainbow colored feathers with exotic iridescence
From the heavens of imagination
Swift is the hummingbird in tantalizing spring
Choreographing toward sweet nectar near the river stream

High hovers the male
On a dive from above
Slicing through the winds
From a harbor known not of

Natural Light

Beautiful as the stars
In the night of the open sky
With a gorgeousness from the heavens
Magnetic to the human eye
With a sparkling existence
God sprinkled upon the sky
As we marvel from below
At the embellishments held high
Bright was her personality
With the warmth of sunshine
In her actions was compassion
And unmistakably natural light

Her Smile

Her smile
Her smile
Epitomizes gorgeousness
Ooh would I love to chaperone you to my fortress miss
It's the beauty of the action
That makes me love to exist
The thought levitates my mind to pure bliss
As I drift

My imagination grips an
Overwhelming sensation
Of Aqua fresh mint
From one kiss
I wish

The expression of your face
Is like an orchestration of grace
From a goddess
It brings my mind to a peaceful place

Don't be modest
It's a gift to you
From you
The type of smile a man could wake up to

My encouragement
Yes
I'm good with the gift of gab and jokes
But alone
Making you laugh is nourishment and hope

Motivational Quotes

For humanity
And positivity
Your majesty
It was a blessing to have you give to me
Your smile

Amazing

So lovely
She is
So beautiful
From the crown of her head
To her toe cuticles
She is
Amazing

Her touch
Her eyes
Her laugh
Her cries
The softness of her lips
Her hips
Her thighs
With the motions of compassion
From the song that she sings
She strikes me as a goddess
Much more than a queen
Her intelligence
Her eloquence
From the most beautiful dream
Creating trails of love leading to the heart of this human being
She is
Amazing

The Beauty of Life

The beauty of life
Is the bringing of so many colors
The hug of the warm hearted
The kiss of the two lovers
The bond of the two brothers
With nothing but each other
Through the manifestation of each thought
My heart flutters
The nourishment of a mother
Breastfeeding an infant
To the heart of the peaceful warrior
That darkened to be relentless
From the elegance of the butterfly
To delicately land
At the tip of the imagination
And In the palm of your hand

Your Flowers

Your flowers
Freshly grown
From Mother Nature's spring
With the beauty of life's rose
To the florescent snows of winter's being

Peruvian Lilies
Fresh jokes and sillies
Of compassion letting you know that I care
So I retrieve for you
Your flowers

With tender love and care
You are a rarity
With colorful speech from out of the parrot's beak

To bring clarity
Share with me these moments to create a botanical garden

Never to let our hearts harden
As we landscape the yard with
Seeds of faith
Hugs and be safes
Just hearing your voice is a blessing
Reminds me of heaven
Aware the gift to me is your presence
So grateful to share this
Moment
Smell the fragrance
Of the essence

Motivational Quotes

I present to you
Your flowers

Ubiquitous Poetry

CHANGE

There is no race.

We are all in the same place.

The soul is colorblind.

It is only us.

We are one.

--Jawusky

Motivational Quotes

The Brightest Treasure

In the vastness of darkness lies the brightest treasure
As if they have somewhat of a connection
A bond or an awareness of existence

Like everything that glitters isn't gold
But it still glitters

There are many walks of life but they are all life

In a sea of togetherness
The world is an abundant mixture
With a selection of streams to sip from the flow of Life's river

Balance

What's done in the darkness
Will come to the light

As negative to a positive
And a yin to a yang
Is the insight of what's left
To the duality of what's right

***

Never give up.
Be persistent.
Persistence
can change your existence
in an instance.

--Jawusky

***

Last Cigarette

The life
The emotion
The mind
The action
The things that we may do
As creatures of habit
I pay no mind to the cigarette as I grab it
And within that motion
Holds the challenge

The deeper I fall
On my quest for balance
The taller I stand up
To the burden I've dragged in
Until I find myself gasping for breath
Driving my habitual ways fearlessly
The hole gets deeper and deeper

So I contemplate as I sit
Until I catch the correct notion
To run with as I quit
I pray that I reposition
the order in which my thoughts exist
In a tug of war with the flesh
May this be my last cigarette

POWER

Try your best.
Face new things.
You may be greater than you imagined.
Never underestimate your ability.
You have greatness within you.
You are powerful.

--Jawusky

God Take the Wheel

Standing strong in adversity and moving forward pass the still
Takes courage of all things
When you let God take the wheel

Sometimes you may get tired
Energy-less and somewhat ill
But never disbelieve
Through these emotions you may feel
Let God take the wheel

God will do the rest
 if you're willing to do the first
As if the first were the last
This too shall pass

All of the greatest became from not giving up through trying times
Just when they thought they would die
They would develop into butterflies
Then naturally
They began to fly

This life is a rollercoaster
Strap up and enjoy the ride
Believe but never be naive
Let God be your guide
Let God drive

I Encourage You

I encourage you to be unique
Through compassion as you speak
From the boundlessness of imagination
Out of beautiful thoughts you may be
A master piecing a work of art
For a garden of souls to see
And the people of earth may believe
I am you and you are me
As we paint the magnum opus of eternity
I encourage you to be

Motivational Quotes

The Power of the Subconscious Mind

The power of the subconscious mind
Calm your thoughts
As we travel through time
Thoughts are plentiful
And abundant indeed
Seeing is believing
Impressionable as can be
From my feelings and my thoughts
To the action I conceive
Oh how my subconscious mind follows me
The power of the subconscious mind

PERCEPTION

Everything is everything

As anything is plenty

Like making something

from nothing

Or turning something

into nothing

with perception

--Jawusky

Motivational Quotes

Perception

Noised by the ring from out of a deep slumber
Startled from out of his warm comfy he awakes
"Why? Why me?" said the frown upon his face
13 minutes before the departure of the pace bus

Startled by footsteps and loud conversation
Where they catch the pace bus throughout the day
where he awakens
Looked down upon in disgrace and dismay
And still he arises with a smile upon his face

***

The Inevitable

There is a light
That continues to shine
Brightly on the other side
Too bright for eyes

As I take a look inside my mind
I realize you can try
But rather or not you choose or decide
It's inevitable

The Baby's Imagination

Pure
As the waters of spring
Without a drop of fluoride
Is a baby's imagination
With love
As its tour guide

Tender
As an embryo
Manifested
Through mother's womb
Curiosity paints the darkness
With stars and a crescent moon

Rock
A bye baby
With the sweetest
Of sweet dreams
A child's imagination
Is the most impressionable thing

Motivational Quotes

***

It's not always about the camera

you choose.

It could be about your lens of preference.

View your life

through a different lens

and you may change

your perception.

--Jawusky

***

See What I See

Maybe if you look in my eyes
You can see what I see
Have mercy upon my actions
And not criticize my belief
Maybe I'd understand you better
If we happened to switch shoes
On the path of self-forgiveness
Forgiving me is forgiving you
From the mentally physically and spiritually abused
To the lack of compassion
Towards the mind of the misused
If you were in my shoes
Maybe you'd feel like me
And if you could look through my eyes
Maybe you'd see what I see

An Engulfed Surface

I can now see clearly
As the water sits still
The world becomes visible
I realize I don't see
But I feel
What do we really know
Where do we really go
If we are all that becomes
Down the river that flows
What is peace to the lion
Is horror to the gazelle
Letters seen by the eyes
To the blind man's braille
With the balance of an angelic ballerina
Thoughts linger through my observance
The road traveled was small
Surrounded by the dark pit
Of an engulfed surface

LIFE

Everyone has their own personal method

on how to take life.

You can only hope to share similar views

being that there is only one you.

--Jawusky

Life

Some things and feelings
Just can't be explained
Somewhat of an overwhelming existence
Which can't be contained

Fluctuations of energy
That waver back n' forth
This life can be a cave
For you to carry a torch

Oil lamps for illumination
Along the path and conquest
On the side the others scream
At the illusion of darkness

Shine light upon this road
We all must take
With the faith to continue on with the whole staircase

The Confusion

When it feels so good
But it seems so wrong
The body won't let go
Of what the mind holds on

When it feels so bad
But it seems so right
It may be a bit difficult
To decipher day from night

Motivational Quotes

***

*Life is art and art is life. Paint
your life one day at a time.*

***

*Life is a song.
Each action is a sound.
Create your own melody to existence.*

--Jawusky

***

The Calm after the Storm

The body becomes at ease
At the feel of the smooth breeze
Massaging the shell into relaxation and euphoric bliss
Gray clouds fade away into the remainder of the day

As life draws you close
To kiss you gently
Upon the lips
Everything is okay

Birds begin where they left off
Dancing from damp limb to damp limb
Singing melodies of glee
Knitted by a joyous faith and new life

The smell of rain submerged in deep soils fills the air
Inhaled deeply into a brain cultivating the growth of the flower of life
Exhaling into the warmth of sunlight without a care

Motivational Quotes

Life's Music

Sound and rhythm
The power of perception
The babies that cry
Even the tears from your eyes

The waves in the ocean
Crash upon the shore
Like the water you pour
Sends back the vibration for
Ears to hear
And eyes to see
Sometimes the sound is deep as the ocean floor

The sounds of the wind
In the open sky
When I
Float and soar music makes me high
War cries of existence
Sing songs of worry
From sad faces
To the scent of a woman's fragrance

The smell of the wonderful vibration is like
Music to my nose
The feeling is the amazement
Ups and downs
Rounds and rounds
We move in colors and sounds of mathematics
The sounds of the mind with emotion added equals action
Let's color the town in an artistic fashion

Ubiquitous Poetry

And let the whole city feel it

Through sight and vibration
From its own cognition
Through visual translation

Because color is sound
And vibration is movement
As we continue to feel
Through the rhythm of life's music

Motivational Quotes

***

As I identify my emotions and monitor my thoughts,
I continue to select from this touch screen called life.

***

The water is the blood
The seed is the brain
The roots are the veins
The torso is the bark
With arms and legs as limbs
– The tree of life –

***

Go into it with faith. Dance with life into the twilights of eternity.

***

Your life isn't going to live itself.
That's your job.
Each day is a page to create in your book of life.

--Jawusky

***

TO BE

Be positive.

Be a lovingly brilliant light of nobility.

Be all the greatness you can.

But whatever you do,

Don't be afraid to be.

-Jawusky

Be Happy

Positive as natural light
Shined upon imagination
For the realistic feel
Of the most joyous sensation
Greeted by the genuine smile of happiness
In a playful friendship with eternity and harmless laughter

So what have we
I glow wherever I go
And can be
I am as I choose
To be
Nothing less
Than happy

Feel it
From your toes throughout your crown
Blasting
Through the beautiful image of life
Feel the vision of happiness
Be happy

I am Poetry

Life is such poetry
From everything we see
To the emotions that we feel
As still waters run deep
The breeze of the open sea
In the waters of the nearest creek
The illusion of the reflection I see
Is poetry

Motivational Quotes

***

*You know you're on the right track,
when you're too busy to realize
someone is competing with you
in a race to the top.
Because unknowingly,
the top is an illusion.*

--Jawusky

***

Watch… For What May Come

Watch what you hear
Then watch what you think
Examine what you see
And be careful what you speak
Watch the way you feel
And what causes the emotion
Stay centered and well balanced
For what may come to be

Motivational Quotes

***

*I feel as if I am highly artistic
because I accept everyone else's creative ability
without judgment.
That way I can co relate with more walks of life
and paint pictures we can all relate to.
-Jawusky*

***

Black Sheep

Exiled from the norm was the calm in the storm that I am
On an open canvas lies the mark of the black sheep
Faded to a black sheet
The white out splats free

I take notes of sorrow
To refill the hollow in trust
The heart of hopelessness that beats
That's me

The magic in the breath
Of the fresh unseen
Refreshing as a sip
From a cup of black tea
As written
It shall be done
When they say it can't be
Signed
sealed the untouchable
Long live the black sheep

Dancing in the Rain

A leap into the waters
Where destiny meets fate
A love being boggled
In which it cannot escape

Each splash of melodies
Sound above the terrain
I was once found crazily sane
Dancing in the rain

Sweet sounds of euphoria
Cleanse the soul of its stain
From clouds of a joyous pain
Being rinsed of its shame

Creating magic in time
With a choreography unexplained
I was once found crazily sane
Dancing in the rain

The Aurora Borealis

I am the Aurora Borealis
That shall leave
Only to return
In a sight never to be imagined
The beauty of cosmic souls
And universal spirits dancing
And prancing through the sky
Laughing above the royal palace

I am the Aurora Borealis

The astounding
Enigmatic
In a sight yet to be challenged
And a mystery yet to be unraveled
Behind these unlocked magics
A phenomenal presentation of these universal fabrics

I am the Aurora Borealis

Motivational Quotes

***

There is always something
new under the sun
and that's you.
So the more comfortable you are
with being yourself,
the better you get
at presenting what's new.

--Jawusky

***

Be Free

Be yourself
Be free
Like a bird in the open sky
Like lava exceeding its peak
With the flow of all streams
And the serenity and peace
Of the sound of the water
Flowing easily in the creek
Like a fish in the sea
Or a cougar in the mountains
A deer in the forest reserve
In what ways can I explain
The feelings beyond words
The clouds that fade away
To display the sky's canvas
The painter of imagination
With a vision
That's everlasting
The grasshopper in the field
Of the man who goes within
Cutting corners of skyscrapers
By the swiftness of the wind
The ink from an empty pen
Placed upon blank pages
Life and its enlightenment
The feeling and the amazement
Of being free

Motivational Quotes

***

*There is nothing like creating your own life.
It is like putting together a wonderful weekend.
Creativity is such an amazing gift.*

--Jawusky

***

BONUS POEMS

Vampire Queen

The closer she became
The more my nostrils flared
My veins began to bulge
And my heart began to beat for the quench of the thirst for her serum as my
Adrenaline rushed

Only to become prey to her vampiric ways
The deeper she sunk her teeth in me
The weaker I became
A victim to her rain
Vulnerable in the same
Slowly restrained and tamed
As a syringe to the nearest vain
I am drained
I've become a slave
To my vampire queen

Unbreakable Love

You know the light called love when it's felt

It's been attacked
Bruised and burdened
But still shines beyond disbelief
Through the pain it doesn't change
Even through the strain
It stays the same

Saddened clouds drop tears of rain
As the emotion I feel when I try to explain
Of a love so bright
That it knows not of its chains

Catalina

Her island is paradise
Where the harmony is pure
Complemented by magic waters
Her world is of enchantment

With a scape of exotic floral as
The clouds read imagine
In the clear blue sky up above
Jade vines and plumerias welcome you through the scent of love

Her birds chirp of happiness
The spirits of joy listen
Her waters continue glistening
Flowers greet you at the entrance

Ubiquitous Poetry

THE END

About Me

I am a poet and artist in many ways, who loves to be creative and express himself.

I like motivational and self-help books that inspire people to do great work, so I decided to try something new, a book with a motivation/poetry type of theme, where the poems motivate you along with a mixture of quotes you may find useful along your journey.

This book is the beginning of my body of work as writer, and I thank you for tagging along on through this amazing body of artistry with me.

I hope you enjoyed the book, and if you did, please leave a review of it.

I wish you all peace, love, and prosperity. Thank you.

--*Jawusky*

Motivational Quotes

See more of my work on Facebook.

https://www.facebook.com/Ubiquitous-Poetry-Motivational-Quotes-1976234822612872/

On Instagram, search: _iamjawusky

Ubiquitous Poetry